How to Improve Your Nonverbal Communications Skills

Effective Strategies for Enhancing Your Non-Verbal Communication

I0462839

By Meir Liraz

Published by BizMove
www.bizmove.com

Table of Contents

MEIR LIRAZ

1. Introduction

When Demosthenes was asked what was the first part of oratory he answered, "'action"; and which was the second, he replied, "action"; and which was third he still answered, "action." People tend to believe actions more than words!

Have you ever heard anyone say, "His actions spoke so loudly I couldn't hear what he said?" Have you ever wondered whether anyone has said this about you? What we do is a means of communication, subject to interpretation by others. Did you ever stop to think that even failure to act is a way of communicating?

Today, many researchers are concerned with the information sent by communication that is independent of and different from verbal information; namely, the non-verbal communication. Verbal communication is organized by language; non-verbal communication is not.

Communication is the transfer of information from one person to another. Most of us spend about 75 percent of our waking hours communicating our knowledge, thoughts, and ideas to others. However, most of us fail to realize that a great deal of our communication is of a non-verbal form as opposed to the oral and written forms. Non-verbal communication includes facial expressions, eye contact, tone of voice, body posture and motions, and positioning within groups. It may also include the way we wear our clothes or the silence we keep.

In person-to-person communications our messages are sent on two levels simultaneously. If the nonverbal cues and the spoken message are incongruous, the flow of communication is hindered. Right or wrong, the receiver of the communication tends to base the intentions of the sender on the non- verbal cues he receives.

2. Categories and Features

G. W. Porter divides non-verbal communication into four broad categories:

Physical. This is the personal type of communication. It includes facial expressions, tone of voice, sense of touch, sense of smell, and body motions.

Aesthetic. This is the type of communication that takes place through creative expressions: playing instrumental music, dancing, painting and sculpturing.

Signs. This is the mechanical type of communication, which includes the use of signal flags, the 21-gun salute, horns, and sirens.

Symbolic. This is the type of communication that makes use of religious, status, or ego-building symbols. Our concern here will be with what Porter has called the physical method of non-verbal communication.

Knowledge of non-verbal communication is important managers who serve as leaders of organizational "teams," for at least two reasons:

• To function effectively as a team leader the manager must interact with the other members successfully. Non-verbal cues, when interpreted correctly, provide him with one means to do so.

• The team members project attitudes and feelings through non¬-verbal communication. Some personal needs such as approval, growth, achievement, and recognition may be met in effective teams. The extent to which these needs are met is closely related to how perceptive the team leader and team members are to non-verbal communication in themselves and in others on the team.

If the team members show a true awareness to non-verbal cues, the organization will have a better chance to succeed, for it will be an open, honest, and confronting unit. Argyle and his associates have been studying the features of nonverbal communication that provide information to managers and their team members. The following summarizes their findings:

3. Static Features

Distance. The distance one stands from another frequently conveys a non-verbal message. In some cultures it is a sign of attraction, while in others it may reflect status or the intensity of the exchange.

Orientation. People may present themselves in various ways: face-to-face, side-to-side, or even back-to-back. For example, cooperating people are likely to sit side-by-side while competitors frequently face one another.

Posture. Obviously one can be lying down, seated, or standing. These are not the elements of posture that convey messages. Are we slouched or erect ? Are our legs crossed or our arms folded ? Such postures convey a degree of formality and the degree of relaxation in the communication exchange.

Physical Contact. Shaking hands, touching, holding, embracing, pushing, or patting on the back all convey messages. They reflect an element of intimacy or a feeling of (or lack of) attraction.

4. Dynamic Features

Facial Expressions. A smile, frown, raised eyebrow, yawn, and sneer all convey information. Facial expressions continually change during interaction and are monitored constantly by the recipient. There is evidence that the meaning of these expressions may be similar across cultures.

Gestures. One of the most frequently observed, but least understood, cues is a hand movement. Most people use hand movements regularly when talking. While some gestures (e.g., a clenched fist) have universal meanings, most of the others are individually learned and idiosyncratic.

Looking. A major feature of social communication is eye contact. It can convey emotion, signal when to talk or finish, or aversion. The frequency of contact may suggest either interest or boredom.

The above list shows that both static features and dynamic features transmit important information from the sender to the receiver.

Tortoriello, Blott, and DeWine have defined non-verbal communication as:

". . . the exchange of messages primarily through

non-linguistic means, including: kinesics (body language), facial expressions and eye contact, tactile communication, space and territory, environment, paralanguage (vocal but non-linguistic cues), and the use of silence and time."

Let's review these non-linguistic ways of exchanging messages in more detail.

5. Kinesics

Lamb believes the best way to access an executive's managerial potential is not to listen to what he has to say, but to observe what he does when he is saying it. He calls this new behavioral science "movement analysis." Some of the movements and gestures he has analyzed follow:

Forward and Backward Movements. If you extend a hand straight forward during an interview or tend to lean forward, Lamb considers you to be an "operator"- good for an organization requiring an infusion of energy or dramatic change of course.

Vertical Movements. If you tend to draw yourself up to your tallest during the handshake, Lamb considers you to be a "presenter." You are a master at selling yourself or the organization in which you are employed.

Side-to-Side Movements. If you take a lot of space while talking by moving your arms about, you are a good informer and good listener. You are best suited for an organization seeking a better sense of direction. Lamb believes there is a relationship between positioning of the body and movements of the limbs and facial expressions. He has observed harmony between the two. On the other hand, if certain gestures are rehearsed, such as those made to impress others, there is a tendency to separate the posture and the movements. The harmony disappears.

Studies by Lamb also indicate that communication comes about through our degree of body flexibility. If you begin a movement with considerable force and then decelerate, you are considered a "gentle-touch." By contrast, if you are a "pressurizer," you are firm from beginning to end. The accuracy of Lamb's analyses is not fully known. However, it is important that corporation executives are becoming so sensitive to the importance of non-verbal messages that they are hiring consultants, such as Lamb, to analyze non-verbal communications in their organizations.

6. Facial Expressions

Facial expressions usually communicate emotions. The expressions tell the attitudes of the communicator. Researchers have discovered that certain facial areas reveal our emotional state better than others. For example, the eyes tend to reveal happiness or sadness, and even surprise. The lower face also can reveal happiness or surprise; the smile, for example, can communicate friendliness and cooperation. The lower face, brows, and forehead can also reveal anger. Mehrabian believes verbal cues provide 7 percent of the meaning of the message; vocal cues, 38 percent; and facial expressions, 55 percent. This means that, as the receiver of a message, you can rely heavily on the facial expressions of the sender because his expressions are a better indicator of the meaning behind the message than his words.

7. Eye Contact

Eye contact is a direct and powerful form of non-verbal communication. The superior in the organization generally maintains eye contact longer than the subordinate. The direct stare of the sender of the message conveys candor and openness. It elicits a feeling of trust. Downward glances are generally associated with modesty. Eyes rolled upward are associated with fatigue.

Tactile Communication

Communication through touch is obviously non-verbal. Used properly it can create a more direct message than dozens of words; used improperly it can build barriers and cause mistrust. You can easily invade someone's space through this type of communication. If it is used reciprocally, it indicates solidarity; if not used reciprocally, it tends to indicate differences in status. Touch not only facilitates the sending of the message, but the emotional impact of the message as well.

8. Personal Space

Personal space is your "bubble" - the space you place between yourself and others. This invisible boundary becomes apparent only when someone bumps or tries to enter your bubble.

How you identify your personal space and use the environment in which you find yourself influences your ability to send or receive messages. How close do you stand to the one with whom you are communicating ? Where do you sit in the room ? How do you position yourself with respect to others at a meeting ? All of these things affect your level of comfort, and the level of comfort of those receiving your message.

Goldhaber says there are three basic principles that summarize the use of personal space in an organization: The higher your position (status) in the organization,

(a) the more and better space you will have,

(b) the better protected your territory will be, and

(c) the easier it will be to invade the territory of lower-status personnel.

The impact of use of space on the communication process is related directly to the environment in which the space is maintained.

9. Environment

How do you arrange the objects in your environment - the desks, chairs, tables, and bookcases? The design of your office, according to researchers, can greatly affect the communications within it. Some managers divide their offices into personal and impersonal areas. This can improve the communication process if the areas are used for the purposes intended.

Your pecking-order in the organization is frequently determined by such things as the size of your desk, square feet in your office, number of windows in the office, quality of the carpet, and type of paintings (originals or copies) on the wall.

It is obvious that your personal space and environment affect the level of your comfort and your status and facilitate or hinder the communication process.

Paralanguage

Is the content of your message contradicted by the attitude with which you are communicating it? Researchers have found that the tone, pitch, quality of voice, and rate of speaking convey emotions that can be accurately judged regardless of the content of the message. The important thing to gain from this is that the voice is important, not just as the conveyor of the message, but as a complement to the message. As a communicator you should be sensitive to the influence of tone, pitch, and quality of your voice on the interpretation of your message by the receiver.

10. Silence and Time

Silence can be a positive or negative influence in the communications process. It can provide a link between messages or sever relationships. It can create tension and uneasiness or create a peaceful situation. Silence can also be judgmental by indicating favor or disfavor - agreement or disagreement.

For example, suppose a manager finds a couple of his staff members resting.

• If he believes these staff members are basically lazy, the idleness conveys to him that they are "goofing off" and should be given additional assignments.

• If he believes these staff members are self-motivated and good workers, the idleness conveys to him that they are taking a well¬-deserved "break."

• If he is personally insecure, the idleness conveys to him that they are threatening his authority.

Time can be an indicator of status. How long will you give the staff member who wishes to speak to you ? How long will you make him wait to see you ?

Do you maintain a schedule? Is your schedule such that your subordinates must arrange their schedules to suit yours ? In a healthy organization, the manager and his subordinates use time to communicate their mutual respect to each other.

Closing Thoughts

Regardless of your position in the organization it is important for you to develop some sensitivity to nonverbal messages. Cooperation improves as we recognize and respond appropriately to non-verbal cues. Of course you have been aware of non-verbal communications all of your life, but how much thought have you given them?

www.ingramcontent.com/pod-product-compliance
Lightning Source LLC
Chambersburg PA
CBHW072312170526
45158CB00003BA/1289